Getting To Know...

Nature's Children

POLAR BEARS

Caroline Greenland

SCHOLASTIC INC.

New York   Toronto   London   Auckland   Sydney
Mexico City   New Delhi   Hong Kong   Buenos Aires

Facts in Brief

Classification of the Polar Bear

    Class: *Mammalia* (mammals)

    Order: *Carnivora* (meat-eaters)

    Family: *Ursidae* (bear family)

    Genus: *Ursus*

    Species: *Ursus maritimus*

World distribution. Polar Bears live in all lands bordering on the Arctic Ocean.

Habitat. Mainly coastal areas; may move somewhat inland in summer and may winter on ice floes.

Distinctive physical characteristics. Thick creamy-white fur; relatively small head and ears; fur on the soles of its feet.

Habits. Solitary except in mating season; excellent swimmer and hunter; often wanders great distances in search of food.

Diet. Sea animals, including fish, walruses, and especially, seals; some grasses and berries in summer.

Published by Scholastic Inc.
90 Old Sherman Turnpike, Danbury, Connecticut 06816.

SCHOLASTIC and associated logos are trademarks of Scholastic Inc.

ISBN 0-7172-6683-4

Printed in the U.S.A.

Edited by: Elizabeth Grace Zuraw

Photo Rights: Ivy Images

Photo Editor: Nancy Norton

Cover Design: Niemand Design

Have you ever wondered . . .

Do you know which large animal of the North is also known as Nanook, Ice King, and Ice Bear? If you guessed the Polar Bear, you're absolutely right!

Most people have never seen a Polar Bear, except in a zoo. But its nicknames give you a hint about where you'd find this animal in the wild. These massive and powerful white giants are found only where there is lots of ice and snow—in the Far North.

Few animals are equipped to survive the frigid winters of the Far North. But Polar Bears are well adapted to living in the icy cold. In fact, if there were such a thing as a cold-weather olympics, this hardy bear would probably be in the finals for every event— from keeping warm, to hunting and maybe even swimming. Not a bad performance!

Let's find out more about these champions of cold-climate survival.

With its dense coat of white fur, the Polar Bear is well equipped for life in the frigid Far North.

Into the Icy Water

Imagine how surprised a baby Polar Bear must be when it sticks its paw into the icy cold arctic water for the first time. Brrr!

Because Polar Bears sometimes have to swim to hunt, it's important for a Polar Bear cub to learn to swim. But…oh…that water sure is mighty cold.

To get her cubs into the water, a mother Polar Bear flops in first and swims a short distance away. The young cubs look nervous and whimper uncertainly. Finally one of them bellyflops in and swims to its mother. The next cub is not far behind.

Once the cubs have been in the water for a few minutes, they seem to start enjoying themselves. Soon they'll be as much at ease in the water as their mother.

Polar Bears are powerful and tireless swimmers. Stretching their head forward, they paddle with their front legs and steer with their back legs.

Polar Bear Relatives

What do weasels, raccoons, dogs, and bears have in common? They all are distant relatives. But the Polar Bear's closest relatives are the Black and Brown Bears.

The Polar Bear is bigger than most of its relatives. Some huge male Polar Bears weigh as much as a compact car. That's a lot of bear! An average-size adult male would tip the scales at 1,100 pounds (500 kilograms). The females are considerably smaller, weighing about 450 pounds (200 kilograms).

A female Polar Bear is called a *sow*. A male Polar Bear is called a *boar*.

Black Bear

Grizzly Bear

Polar Bear

If you stood next to this Polar Bear, your head might just about reach its paw. A full-grown male bear is 8-11 feet (2.4-3.4 meters) tall. Females are about 6 feet (1.8 meters).

Polar Bear Country

Imagine visiting a place where there are no trees or grass, only ice and snow. And it's dark, even though it's the middle of the day. The temperature is far below freezing, and an icy wind cuts right through your clothes.

Feeling chilly? You've just taken an imaginary trip to Polar Bear country in the winter.

Polar Bears live in the lands surrounding the Arctic Ocean, the body of water that covers the North Pole. Since their main food is seal, they spend much of their time near the coast where seals live.

In the summer the Arctic is a very different place. The snow and ice melt, and the land is covered with many kinds of plants and colorful flowers. During the summer some Polar Bears move inland and feast on plants, berries, and small animals, but most follow the seals as they travel even farther north in search of fish.

Later, as winter approaches again, the seals and Polar Bears *migrate,* or move, back to their more southerly homes.

Polar Bear Capital of the World

Churchill, a town on Hudson Bay in Canada's Manitoba province, is famous for its Polar Bear visitors. In winter, many Polar Bears live on the ice of northern Hudson Bay. As the ice breaks up, some of the bears ride the big chunks and end up on the bay's southern shore. By then it's summer and too warm for the bears, so they start migrating north. They trek about 800 miles (1,287 kilometers) to the exact place where they know the bay will soon freeze again: the town of Churchill.

During October and November, the bears make themselves at home in the area. Mostly they roam the nearby wilderness in search of food, or stay near the water, waiting for it to freeze. The residents of Churchill are fond of their visitors, but if the bears get too close to their houses, the animals are caught, put into "bear jail," and then removed by helicopter.

Many people go to Churchill, Manitoba, every year to see the Polar Bears. Tundra buggies, *like the one shown here, are special vehicles with huge wheels that take tourists to view the animals.*

Cold Weather Comfort

When you look at a roly-poly Polar Bear, you might think it's wearing one heavy fur coat, but actually it's wearing two. It has a thick, short coat of underhair next to its skin to trap body-warmed air. Covering this is a longer outer coat of shiny coarse *guard hairs,* which repel water, ice, and snow like a raincoat. When a Polar Bear comes out of the water, it shakes itself off like a huge furry dog to rid its coat of icy water.

Under a Polar Bear's skin is a layer of fat up to 3.5 inches (9 centimeters) thick. This layer of fat acts as *insulation,* protection to keep the cold out.

A Polar Bear's coat is perfectly designed for cold weather. Fur covers every inch of the animal's body except its nose!

No Cold Toes

Have you ever noticed how your hands, feet, ears, and nose are the first parts of your body to get cold when you're playing outdoors on a frosty winter day? Well, animals are like that, too. They feel the cold first in those same parts of their bodies, especially in their ears. But Polar Bears' furry ears are very small and this means they lose less heat into the frosty air. And to keep its feet warm, the Polar Bear has a thick covering of fur on the soles of its feet. These built-in slippers also keep the bear from skidding on ice.

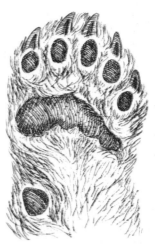

Front paw

Back paw

A Polar Bear's short, furry ears are ideally suited for cold weather. They let less body heat escape than long ears would.

17

Keeping Cool

The Polar Bear's cold-weather outfit keeps it comfortable and warm—sometimes *too* warm. In the summer, the Polar Bear sheds its heavy winter coat. But even so, it sometimes has a problem cooling off. A hot bear solves this problem by digging itself a summer *den,* or home. It digs deep into the ground, down to where the soil is still frozen. As its body heat melts the frozen ground, the bear digs down a little deeper. The bear uses this "bear refrigerator" whenever it needs to cool off.

A Polar Bear's white coat makes it quite visible against the summer landscape. Fortunately, the bear has little need to worry about being spotted—it has few enemies.

Walk Like a Bear

Try walking on all fours by placing your hands and feet flat on the ground at each step. And point your fingers and toes slightly inward rather than straight ahead.

How did you do? Probably not too well. But even though it might not be easy for you, a Polar Bear can get around just fine with this flat-footed, pigeon-toed walk. A Polar Bear often covers a large hunting territory in a day with its rather clumsy-looking, lumbering walk. And if need be, this bear can even gallop over short distances at speeds of up to 35 miles (56 kilometers) per hour.

They may have a slow and ponderous gait, but Polar Bears can cover a lot of territory in a day.

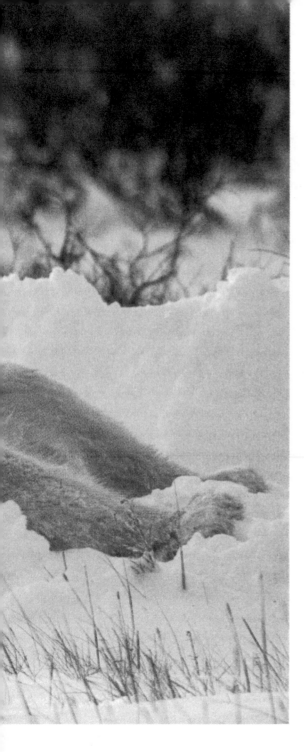

A Bear Slide

The ice- and snow-covered land where the Polar Bear lives is mostly flat. But sometimes miniature mountains of ice and snow form. The Polar Bear, a good climber, can easily get up these snow hills—but getting back down can be a problem.

Polar Bears have come up with two tricks to help them move downhill. One is to walk slowly, using their front legs as brakes. The other is simply to lie down and slide on their bellies, headfirst! Sounds like fun, doesn't it?—a kind of Arctic version of the slides you see in playgrounds.

Sometimes, Polar Bear play is just stretching out and lying lazily in the snow.

Web-footed Super Swimmers

In snow, the Polar Bear's wide feet act like snowshoes, and keep the animal on top of the snow. But the bear's front feet are also slightly webbed, like a duck's, making the feet excellent swimming flippers. Polar Bears wouldn't win any ribbons for speed swimming, but they might win a swimming marathon. If necessary, they can dog-paddle tirelessly for more than 60 miles (100 kilometers) at one stretch! Their shoulder and neck muscles are highly developed, and their streamlined body, which is narrower in the front than the back, cuts easily through the water, a bit like the bow of a boat. When swimming, a Polar Bear uses its front feet as paddles. The back feet are used to steer.

A Polar Bear's large front feet make perfect paddles for swimming.

Underwater Swimmer

Sometimes a Polar Bear dives underwater to chase a seal or avoid a chunk of floating ice. But it doesn't have to worry about getting water up its nose. Polar Bears can close their nostrils as tightly as if they were wearing nose-plugs! And they can hold their breath to stay underwater for as long as two minutes.

Polar Bears are at home in the water. Next time you visit the zoo, watch the Polar Bears swimming in their pool. With all that splashing and diving, it's plain to see that they like to swim.

Breaking the water with a mighty splash, a Polar Bear comes up for air during a seal hunt.

Sharp Eyes, Sharp Nose

Polar Bears have good eyesight, which helps them while hunting. They often stand up on their hind legs to get a better view of what's going on around them. But it's the Polar Bear's sense of smell that is the keenest. It can help the bear locate seals and other animals more than 10 miles (16 kilometers) away!

A sharp sense of sight and smell is important for a Polar Bear because it lives in a barren land where food is scarce most of the year. A Polar Bear can't afford to miss spotting food.

Opposite page: *The Polar Bear technically is an* omnivore, *an animal that eats both plants and flesh. But because it prefers flesh, the Polar Bear is considered a* carnivore, *an animal that eats only flesh.*

Northern Hunters

Because the Polar Bear needs to eat an average of 9 pounds (4 kilograms) of meat a day, it spends a lot of time hunting. Seals are the Polar Bear's favorite food, but seals are not easy to catch. They're fast-moving, clever, and cautious. To catch enough seals to survive, the Polar Bear has some clever hunting techniques.

In winter, seals hunt for fish by swimming under the ice. To catch a seal, a Polar Bear waits patiently near one of the holes in the ice where seals come up to breathe. The bear knows that if it waits long enough, a seal will poke its head up through this breathing hole to take a gulp of air. When this happens, the Polar Bear tries to grab the seal. If it misses, the bear will often move to a new hole and begin its long wait all over again.

Another hunting trick is to watch for a seal sunning itself on the ice. When a bear spots one, it crouches down low to the ground and begins slowly to creep up on the unsuspecting seal. A bear's white coat makes perfect *camouflage*, it blends in with its surroundings so that the bear is hard to spot. The bear also takes advantage of any big ice chunks or bumps in the ground to hide behind. When the bear is close enough to surprise the seal, it pounces!

A Polar Bear waits for a seal to surface for air at an opening in the ice. If the bear is fast enough, it'll grab the seal and haul it out for a prized dinner.

A Polar Bear may also swim quietly up to seals dozing on an *ice floe,* large pieces of floating ice, and leap out of the water at them. However difficult this feat may sound, it seems to pose no problem for the powerful Polar Bear.

Keep Your Distance

Because of its size and strength, the Polar Bear has few enemies. However, it must watch out for at least two predators: walruses and Killer Whales. *Predators* are animals that hunt other animals for food.

As a rule, Polar Bears also usually avoid each other's company, so they seldom get close enough to fight. In fact, when two bears have to pass each other on the ice, they often keep a distance between them that's equal to the length of a football field! Now that's not exactly friendly.

During the summer *mating season,* the time of year during which animals come together to produce young, male Polar Bears may hurt or even kill each other when fighting about who is going to be a female's mate.

Starting a Family

When a female Polar Bear is four or five years old, she is ready to start a family. From late March to early June, she is approached by many males. A male bear wins a female by fighting other males to prove his strength. Females mate only with the largest and strongest males.

The couple stays together for days or even weeks. This is the only time male and female Polar Bears are found together.

During mating season, a male and female Polar Bear are quite playful with each other.

A Warm, Cozy Den

By mid-October the sow begins her search for a place to dig a den. She knows instinctively that arctic winds will soon be howling and she must find a warm place to have her babies.

She looks for a hill that faces south and is covered with plenty of snow. Here she digs out a shallow den. The sow is careful to make the den itself higher than the entrance hole so that water from melting snow runs out of the shelter, and warm air, which rises, does not escape. The den never gets toasty warm, but it's certainly warmer than the frosty air outside.

Sometimes if the weather turns bitterly cold, male Polar Bears may take shelter in a quickly dug den. They never enter another bear's den. But most of the winter, males wander in search of food and they even sleep outdoors.

Between November and early January, the Polar Bear mother gives birth. Most often she'll have two cubs, but sometimes only one or as many as four.

Opposite page:
A mother bear digs a den in a hill that faces south. That way, after the long dark Arctic winter, the sun's warm rays in spring help open the den's entrance.

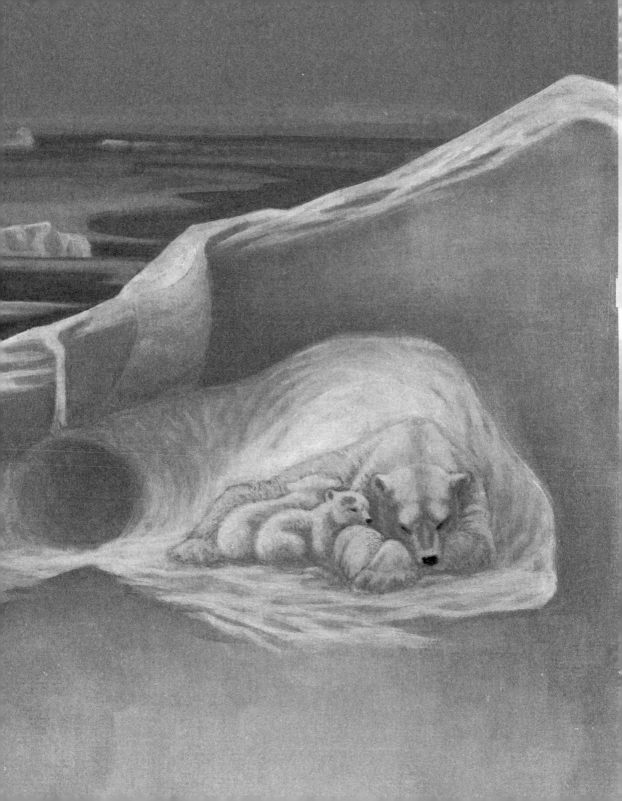

Bear Babies

How tiny and helpless the cubs are when they're born! Their huge mother must take care that she doesn't crush them by accident. The newborn cubs, hairless and deaf, are only about the size of guinea pigs. Their eyes don't open until they're at least two weeks old.

The cubs spend the first two months of their lives in the warm den with their mother. During this period the cubs *nurse,* they drink milk from their mother's body.

Nourished by their mother's rich milk, the cubs grow quickly. By March they have a white woolly coat and weigh about 22 pounds (10 kilograms). Now mother and cubs are ready to leave the protection of their winter home for short hunting trips to the sea. The female is very hungry because she hasn't eaten the entire time she's been in the den. She's lived on the fat stored in her body.

Once Polar Bear babies are old enough to leave their den, they have to start learning the skills they'll need for surviving in their Arctic surroundings.

Hunting and Swimming Lessons

While their mother catches seals, the Polar Bear cubs stay close by and watch her carefully. Although they will still nurse for some time, they eventually must catch seals for themselves. By watching their mother, the cubs learn how to sneak up on seals and they practice other important hunting skills.

The mother Polar Bear also encourages her cubs to practice swimming. Soon they feel quite at home in the icy water. While the cubs are going through this learning stage, the Inuit, the native Eskimo people of North America, call them "ah tik tok." The words mean "those that go down to the sea."

A sow has her babies about eight months after mating. The family group stays together up to two years. The sow usually has cubs every three years.

Furry Hitchhikers

The sow is a good mother, lavishing great care and attention on her little cubs. While traveling across the snow and ice, she often lies down to allow her little ones to nurse or to climb up on her to warm their feet. Or, if they grow tired while swimming, she lets them climb up on her back, piggy-back style. Young cubs have even been seen hitching a ride by grabbing onto their mother's tail with their mouths!

While a mother Polar Bear takes a little nap, her cubs play on her soft warm body. If any danger presented itself, however, the sow would be up in a moment to protect her babies.

The Cubs Grow Up

By the time the cubs are a year old, they've grown to about the size of a St. Bernard dog. But they still need their mother to protect them. To wolves and adult Polar Bears, bear cubs are *prey,* animals hunted for food.

The cubs stay with their mother until they are one and a half years old, or even older. Then, grown to a sturdy weight of about 200 pounds (90 kilograms), each cub will start life on its own.

To us a young Polar Bear's first few years on its own may seem like a cold and lonely life. The young bear often wanders by itself in the frozen North, rarely even seeing another Polar Bear. But Polar Bears prefer to live alone and they seem to enjoy wandering through the snowy arctic world. If they have learned their hunting skills well, they may live to be 20-30 years old and have several families of their own.

Words To Know

Boar The male of various kinds of animals, including the Polar Bear.

Camouflage Coloring and markings on an animal that blend in with its surroundings.

Carnivore An animal that eats flesh.

Den An animal home.

Guard hairs Long coarse hairs that make up the outer layer of a Polar Bear's coat.

Ice floe Very large pieces of floating ice.

Insulation A material, such as fur or fat, that helps an animal keep heat in when it is cold.

Mate To come together to produce young.

Mating season The time of year during which animals mate.

Migrate Travel from one region to another for feeding or breeding.

Nurse To drink milk from a mother's body.

Omnivore An animal that eats both plants and flesh.

Predator An animal that lives by hunting other animals for food.

Prey An animal hunted by another animal for food.

Sow The female of various kinds of animals, including the Polar Bear.

Tundra buggy A special tall vehicle with huge wheels used for taking tourists to see the Polar Bears around Churchill, Manitoba.

Index

PHOTO CREDITS
Cover: Lynn & Donna Rogers, *Ivy Images.* **Interiors:** *Valan Photos:* Wayne Lankinen, 4, 9, 16, 19, 28, 35; Stephen J. Krasemann, 10; Frank E. Johnson, 21; J. A. Wilkinson, 26; Dr. A. Farquhar, 43. */Ivy Images:* Robert R. Taylor, 7. /Wayne Lankinen, 13, 32. /Bill Ivy, 15. /Canada In Stock / Ivy Images: Gary Crandall, 22. /Hot Shots / Ivy Images: J. D. Taylor, 25. /Fred Bruemmer, 31. /Wayne Lynch, 36, 41, 45.

Getting To Know...

Nature's Children

SKUNKS

Laima Dingwall

SCHOLASTIC INC.

New York   Toronto   London   Auckland   Sydney
Mexico City   New Delhi   Hong Kong   Buenos Aires

Facts in Brief

Classification of the Striped Skunk

    Class: *Mammalia* (mammals)

    Order: *Carnivora* (meat-eaters)

    Family: *Mustelidae* (weasel family)

    Genus: *Mephitis* (terrible smell)

    Species: *Mephitis mephitis*

World distribution. Exclusive to North America. Closely related species found in various areas of North, Central, and South America.

Habitat. Areas of mixed forest and grassland are the preferred habitat, but the Striped Skunk is very adaptable, and can even be found in densely populated areas.

Distinctive physical characteristics. Shiny black fur with white stripe on face and two down the back; foul-smelling musk that can be sprayed; long straight claws suited for digging.

Habits. Active mainly at night; sprays its musk when angered or threatened; in the North, spends most of the winter inside den, but is not a true hibernator.

Published by Scholastic Inc.
90 Old Sherman Turnpike, Danbury, Connecticut 06816.

SCHOLASTIC and associated logos are trademarks of Scholastic Inc.

ISBN 0-7172-6683-4
Printed in the U.S.A.

Edited by: Elizabeth Grace Zuraw
Photo Rights: Ivy Images
Photo Editor: Nancy Norton
Cover Design: Niemand Design

Have you ever wondered . . .

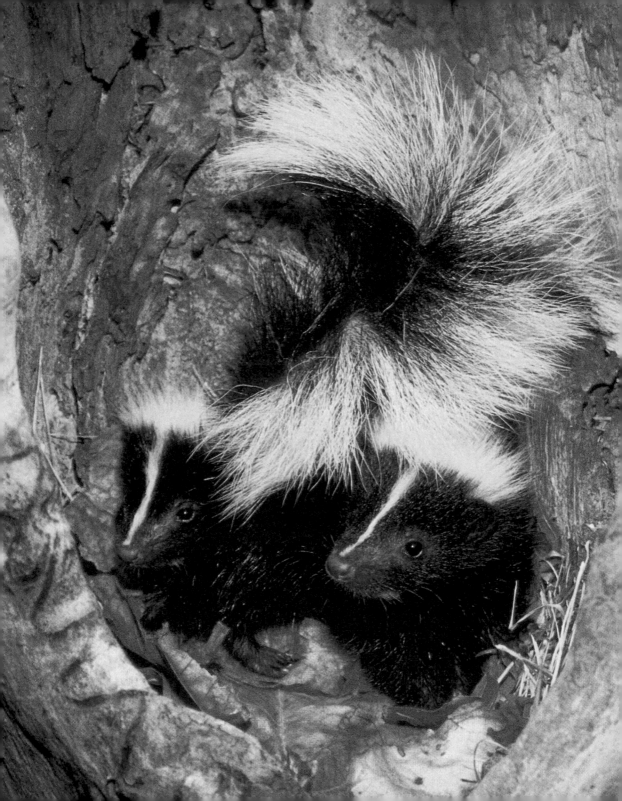

If you saw these cuddly little balls of black-and-white fluff, you might want to pick them up and hug them. But watch out! These eight-week-old babies are skunks. Though they may be cute and small, their smell is mighty powerful—and definitely something you'll want to avoid.

But there's more to skunks than their foul odor. They're handsome and mild-mannered animals. And believe it or not, skunks prefer to be left alone. They'd much rather *not* cause a big stink!

Born in the spring, young skunks snuggle in the grass-lined home prepared by their mother.

Skunk Country

Opposite page:
The skunks found in North America are about the size of a cat, but their legs are shorter and their tails much bushier. Some of a skunk's tail hairs are several inches long.

Wherever you live in North America, you probably don't live far from one or another kind of skunk. Some skunks make their home in hot, dry deserts, and others in forests and along river valleys. Many live on farmland, where there's a plentiful supply of food available.

You might even find some skunks in city backyards. If you do, treat them with respect. Remember: The skunk may look harmless, but its spray is potent.

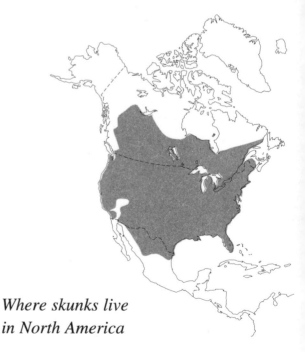

Where skunks live in North America

Skunks, Skunks...

Four different kinds of skunks live in North America: the Hog-nosed, the Hooded, the Spotted, and the Striped.

Hog-nosed Skunks live in the southwestern United States. They got their name because of—what else—their hog-like noses. They use these wide hairless snouts much the way a pig does, to root or dig out food from the ground.

Scientists know very little about the Hooded Skunk, which lives in the deserts of the southwestern United States. But they do know that it has the longest tail of all skunks—up to 15 inches (38 centimeters)—and has very long hair around its neck. This long hair looks rather like a hood—so now you know how the Hooded Skunk got its name!

It's easy to see how the Hog-nosed Skunk got its name. Its pig-like snout is used to dig for food.

...And More Skunks

Spotted Skunks, which live in most of the United States and parts of Canada, are the smallest of all the skunks and the only tree climbers. They have an unusual way of spraying enemies. Instead of just lifting their tails, they do a handstand on their front feet and often spray from that position.

The most common skunk of all is the Striped Skunk. It lives in most parts of North America. Striped skunks are about the size of house cats, except they have short, stubby legs. Let's take a closer look at these well-known skunks.

Opposite page: The boldly-patterned Spotted Skunk has white spots and stripes all over its body. Its tail is a long white plume.

Striped Skunk

Spotted Skunk

10

One Big Happy Family

Early North American settlers called the skunk "polecat" because it reminded them of a small, furry animal that lives in Europe. Even today many people still call the skunk by this name.

It's not surprising that people get the skunk and the polecat mixed up. They both belong to the weasel family. Other North American weasels include the River Otter, Sea Otter, mink, fisher, ermine, and wolverine.

Weasels come in many sizes and colors, but they all have one thing in common. They all produce *musk,* a strong-smelling substance found in glands at the base of their tail. A *gland* is a part of an animal's body that makes and gives out a substance. Can you guess which member of the weasel family makes the worst smell of all? If you answered the skunk, you're right on target.

The scientific name for a Striped Skunk, shown here, is Mephitis mephitis. *This is Latin for "terrible smell, terrible smell."*

Sniff, Sniff

How would you describe the smell of a skunk's spray? One *naturalist*—a person who studies animals and plants—said that the spray smells like strong ammonia, garlic, burning sulphur, sewer gas, and perfume musk all mixed up together. Pheww!

A skunk's spray smells so bad that it makes some people and animals sick. If the musk is sprayed on skin or eyes, it stings and burns. It may even cause blindness for a few minutes. But though the unpleasant effects of being sprayed by a skunk don't last long, animals learn from experience to get out of the way of a skunk when they see its tail go up.

Though small in size, the skunk has a mighty defense system—its odor. The horrible smell keeps even large animals at a safe distance.

Warning Signals

A skunk doesn't spray its foul-smelling musk on every animal or person that it meets. Its glands hold only about one tablespoon of musk—enough for five or six sprays a week. For that reason, the skunk saves its secret weapon only for real emergencies.

Even if an enemy gets too close and the skunk becomes frightened or annoyed, it still doesn't automatically spray. Usually it warns the intruder first. How? It lowers its head and hisses and growls. Then it stamps its front feet one at a time and rakes the ground with its feet like a miniature bull. Finally, it waves its bushy tail in warning.

A lowered head, a threatening growl, and front feet clawing at the ground—these are a skunk's clear warning signals to back off.

Ready, Steady, Spray

If all its warnings don't scare the enemy away, the skunk gets ready to spray. It arches its back, lifts its tail, and bends its body into a U-shaped position so that its head and tail both point toward the intruder. Then—squirt!—it lets its spray fly from its tail glands.

When a skunk fires its spray, it lifts its tail high to keep the scent off its own fur. Other animals aren't so lucky. A skunk can score a direct hit with its spray a car's length away. Once the spray is in the air, it breaks up into a fine mist that sticks and clings to fur and clothing. This smelly mist can spread down-wind for more than half a mile (three-quarters of a kilometer). And the smell can linger for many hours.

This Striped Skunk is getting ready to spray. That's easy to tell because its tail is straight up.

Enemy List

It's not surprising that Striped Skunks have few enemies. Most animals quickly learn not to bother a skunk. But some animals will risk being sprayed in the hope of catching a skunk for dinner. These fearless *predators,* animals that hunt other animals for food, include the Great Horned Owl, coyote, fox, badger, and the fisher.

The owl has better luck than other animals at avoiding the skunk's spray. A Great Horned Owl can swoop down so swiftly and silently that the skunk often doesn't know the owl is there until it's too late. Even the skunk's spray doesn't stop the owl! The smell doesn't seem to bother this bird at all.

A skunk eats a lot of food in the fall to build up a thick layer of fat on its body. During the winter the skunk lives on this stored energy.

Getting Around

The Striped Skunk has a stocky body and short legs. When it walks, it waddles a bit like a duck. But if it has to, the skunk can run in a quick gallop and reach speeds up to 9 miles (14 kilometers) per hour. Because the skunk has small lungs, however, it tires quickly and can keep up that speed for only a short time.

Walking and running aren't the only ways that skunks get around. All skunks are fine swimmers and often dog-paddle across ponds—or perhaps it would be more accurate to say they skunk-paddle!

All Striped Skunks have some white hair on their tail, if only on the tip. And they have two very wide stripes down their back, as well as a thin white stripe in the center of their face.

A Coat that Warms and Warns

A skunk's two-layered fur coat helps keep it warm in cold weather. A thick inner layer of kinky fur acts much like sheep's wool to keep in body heat. An outer layer of extra-long hairs, called *guard hairs,* keeps out the cold and rain.

But the skunk's coat is useful for warning, too. Those bold white stripes on black are easy to recognize. They give other animals a clear message: "Stay away. If not, I'll spray!"

In cold northern regions, a skunk's activities are greatly reduced in winter. But when a skunk does venture out into the cold, its layered fur coat keeps it warm.

Snacking with Skunks

What do skunks eat? Everything and anything.

A skunk's favorite treats are insects—everything from beetles to grubs and grasshoppers. To find these insects, a skunk depends on its keen sense of smell. The skunk usually walks along with its sensitive nose to the ground. That way it can easily sniff out insects and other little creatures living underground or hiding in the grass. A skunk even sneezes several times on these walks to clear its nose and help it smell better!

If a skunk smells insects underground, it digs them out with its front feet. That job is easy because each front foot has five very long, strong claws. Skunks are also fond of eggs and will dig out any turtle or snake eggs they can find.

A goose defends the eggs in its nest from a skunk. Eggs make a tasty snack for a skunk.

The skunk has a very keen sense of hearing, too. If it hears small creatures rustling in the grass, it will pounce on them. Mice, shrews, voles, birds, chipmunks, and even cottontail rabbits are all a skunk's *prey,* animals hunted by other animals for food. Sometimes the skunk feeds on dead animals as well. And if a skunk lives near a pond or marsh, it feasts on frogs, snakes, minnows, lizards, and crayfish.

Skunks also feed on berries, apples, and other fruit, as well as grass, leaves, and buds. Skunks that live in farm country often munch on grains such as corn and barley. But even though skunks eat crops, most farmers like having skunks around. That's because the skunks eat up many of the insects and mice that often destroy farm crops.

A skunk's hearing and smelling are highly developed, but not its vision. A skunk's eyes are very nearsighted and can barely see objects 25 feet (8 meters) away.

Skunk pawprints

Night Feeders, Day Dreamers

Skunks eat at night. As soon as it gets dark, a skunk waddles quietly through its territory looking for food. A *territory* is an area that an animal or group of animals lives in.

The size of a skunk's territory depends on the amount of food in the area. If there is a lot of food, the territory will be small. If food is scarce, the territory is much larger. Usually a skunk's territory is about 10 acres (4 hectares).

Within its territory, a skunk makes a *den,* or home, to sleep in during the day. Sometimes it digs out a *burrow,* a hole in the ground used as a home, or takes over a den abandoned by another animal. And sometimes it sleeps in hollow tree stumps, woodpiles, or under buildings. But whatever its home, a skunk always lines it with dried leaves and grasses to make a cozy nest.

Skunks are nocturnal, *or active mostly at night. But they don't always sleep during the day. If they're hungry they may start to feed at dusk or even in broad daylight.*

Wintertime Skunks

Skunks in southern regions are active year-round. In those areas, the weather stays mild, and the skunk is able to hunt and find food throughout the year. But skunks living farther north *hibernate,* settle down into a kind of deep sleep through the cold weather.

Skunks do not hibernate the way chipmunks and Ground Squirrels do. True hibernators sleep all winter, but skunks wake up from time to time. In fact, a skunk leaves its den on mild winter nights to search for food. But once the weather turns cold again, the skunk crawls back into its den for a few more days of sleep.

A skunk usually dens up alone, but sometimes it shares the den with another skunk. Occasionally two or more whole families snuggle up together.

A skunk often leaves its winter den on mild days to forage for food. With its large claws and 34 razor-sharp teeth, a skunk is well equipped to root for food in the ground.

Mating Time

Skunks *mate,* or come together to produce young, during the warm spells of weather in late February or early March. To find a mate, a male skunk wanders through its territory, traveling several miles (several kilometers) a night. Two males sometimes fight over the same female. But they rarely spray each other.

A male skunk often mates with several female skunks during the mating season. After a female skunk has mated, she may go back to her den to sleep some more.

Skunks are ready to mate by the time they are one year old. After mating, the male does not remain with the female to prepare a den or help raise the young.

Skunk Birthday

In early spring the female skunk gives birth to four to six babies in her grass-lined den. One mother skunk gave birth to 18 babies in the same *litter,* the group of young animals born together. That's a record!

Newborn skunks, called *kits,* are so tiny that you could easily hold two of them in the palm of your hand. They weigh barely 1 ounce (28 grams) each and measure just 4 inches (10 centimeters) from the tip of their noses to the end of their tails. They are born deaf and blind.

The newborn skunks have hardly any hair. But even so, the outline of black-and-white stripes shows faintly in their fine baby hair.

Baby skunks make clicking sounds with their tongues. As they grow older, they start to squeal like a mouse.

Fast Growers

A baby skunk spends its early days in the den with its mother. When it isn't sleeping, it's *nursing,* drinking its mother's milk. It grows quickly. By the time a baby skunk is only one week old, it has doubled its birth weight! By the time it's three weeks old, it's crawling around the den.

There is much play-fighting in the den between the skunk brothers and sisters. When they are a month old, the young skunks practice lifting their tails as if they were about to spray. But nothing happens. They cannot spray their musk until they are about six or seven weeks old. That's when they leave the den and need their secret weapon.

A young skunk stops drinking its mother's milk and starts eating insects when it is six weeks old. But it rarely travels alone until it is three months old.

Skunks on Parade

When a young skunk is ready to leave the den, it doesn't go out alone. Instead, the mother skunk leads it out with its brothers and sisters. The mother skunk is very strict and doesn't let her young ones wander away by themselves. Instead, she leads the way, and the family follows close behind in single file. This way the mother can keep a watchful eye on her babies and protect them from danger.

The young skunks are usually safe near their mother. To protect them, she would never hesitate to spray a predator or any other creature that came too close to her family.

On these outings, the young skunks learn how to hunt for food by watching their mother. She shows them how to dig for grubs and other insects. Soon the young are feasting on insects and sampling berries and tasty plants. And if they're lucky and fast enough, they might even catch a mouse.

Opposite page: *A mother skunk and her young family look like a little parade of black-and-white fur as they wander through a meadow.*

Leaving Home

As the young skunks grow bigger and stronger, they go on longer and longer outings with their mother each night. By the fall, however, the skunk family usually breaks up. The young skunks wander away to find dens of their own. Sometimes one or two of the young skunks stay with their mother until the following spring. Then they, too, are ready to go off by themselves and start families of their own.

By autumn, most young skunks go off by themselves and look for dens of their own.

A Friend After All

The powerful and unpleasant smell of skunks is enough to make people stay away from them. But even though we might not be able to get too close to a skunk, we should be glad that they're around. Why? The skunk's appetite for insects helps control pests that might otherwise destroy farmers' crops.

So the next time you see a skunk waddling through the woods or even at the zoo, think twice about turning up your nose and saying "Pheww!" Remember—there's more to a skunk than its smell.

It has been said that skunks destroy more insects than all other mammals combined.

Words To Know

Burrow   A hole dug by an animal to be used as a home.

Den   Animal home or shelter.

Desert   Hot, dry area with few plants or trees.

Gland   A part of an animal's body that makes and gives out a substance.

Guard hairs   Long, coarse hairs that make up the outer layer of a skunk's coat.

Hibernate   Settle down into a kind of heavy sleep during the winter. When animals hibernate, their breathing and heart rate slow, and their body temperature drops.

Kit   Name of the young of various animals, including the skunk.

Litter   Group of young animals born together.

Mate   To come together to produce young.

Musk   A substance with a strong smell that lasts a long time.

Naturalist   A person who studies animals and plants.

Nocturnal   Active mostly at night.

Nurse   To drink milk from a mother's body.

Predator   An animal that hunts other animals for food.

Prey   An animal hunted by another animal for food.

Territory   Area that an animal or group of animals lives in and often defends from other animals of the same kind.

How can you tell if a skunk has been digging in your yard? There will be small cone-shaped holes in the ground where it has been rooting.

Index

PHOTO CREDITS
Cover: Thomas Kitchin. **Interiors:** Marty Cordano, 4, 8, 23, 31, 35. /Thomas Kitchin, 7, 24, 26.
/*Valan Photos:* Stephen J. Krasemann, 11, 19, 46. /*Ontario Ministry of Natural Resources,* 12.
/Bill Ivy, 15, 16, 20, 37, 42, 44. /*Tom Stack & Associates:* Victoria Hurst, 28. /*Network Stock
Photo File:* Barry Griffiths, 32. /Bruno Kern, 39. /*Ivy Images:* Lynn & Donna Rogers, 40.